O.W. HOLMES JR HIGH
1220 DREXEL DRIVE
DAVIS, CA 95616-2123

D0578261

HIP-HOP

The Black Eyed Peas have worked hard to earn the respect and adoration of fans all over the world. They are one of the most popular groups in hip-hop.

The Black Eyed Peas

E.J. Sanna

Mason Crest Publishers

Black Eyed Peas

Produced by Harding House Publishing Service, Inc.
201 Harding Avenue, Vestal, NY 13850.

MASON CREST PUBLISHERS INC.
370 Reed Road
Broomall, Pennsylvania 19008
(866)MCP-BOOK (toll free)
www.masoncrest.com

Printed in the United States of America

First Printing

9 8 7 6 5 4 3 2 1

Library of Congress Cataloging-in-Publication Data

Sanna, E. J.
  Black Eyed Peas / E. J. Sanna.
     p. cm. — (Hip-hop)
  Includes index.
  ISBN 978-1-4222-0283-8
  ISBN 978-1-4222-0077-3
  1. Black Eyed Peas (Musical group)—Juvenile literature. 2. Rap musicians—
United States—Biography—Juvenile literature. I. Title.
ML3930.B577S36 2008
 782.421649092'2—dc22
[B]
                         2007032956

Contents

Hip-Hop Time Line

1976 Grandmaster Flash and the Furious Five emerge as one of the first battlers and freestylers.

1984 The track "Roxanne Roxanne" sparks the first diss war.

1970s DJ Kool Herc pioneers the use of breaks, isolations, and repeats using two turn-tables.

1988 Hip-hop record sales reach 100 million annually.

1982 Afrika Bambaataa tours Europe in another hip-hop first.

1970s Grafitti artist Vic begins tagging on New York subways.

1980 Rapper Kurtis Blow sells a million records and makes the first nationwide TV appearance for a hip-hop artist.

1985 The film *Krush Groove*, about the rise of Def Jam Records, is released.

1970   1980

1970s The central elements of the hip-hop culture begin to emerge in the Bronx, New York City.

1983 Ice-T releases his first singles, marking the earliest examples of gangsta rap.

1986 Run DMC cover Aerosmith's "Walk this Way" and appear on the cover of *Rolling Stone*.

1979 "Rapper's Delight," by The Sugarhill Gang, goes gold.

1984 *Graffitti Rock*, the first hip-hop television program, premieres.

1974 Afrika Bambaataa organizes the Universal Zulu Nation.

1981 Grandmaster Flash and the Furious Five release *Adventures on the Wheels of Steel*.

1988 MTV premieres *Yo! MTV Raps*.

1989 *Billboard* recognizes rap music as a category.

1993 Snoop Dogg's debut album *Doggystyle* becomes the first hip-hop album to debut at #1.

2003 50 Cent debuts with *Get Rich or Die Tryin*.

2006 The Smithsonian National Museum of American History announces the creation of a new hip-hop exhibition, scheduled to open in two years.

1997 The Notorious B.I.G. is gunned down in Los Angeles.

1990s Hip-hop gains popularity in Europe.

1994 Nas releases *Illmatic*, which becomes the first album to ever receive a five out of five rating from *The Source*.

2004 The first National Hip-Hop Political Convention is held in New Jersey.

2007 Grandmaster Flash and the Furious Five are the first rap artists to be inducted into the Rock and Roll Hall of Fame.

1990   2000

1994 In Puerto Rico, the musical genre that had been called "Dem Bow" or "Underground" now starts to be referred to as "Reggaeton."

2004 Daddy Yankee's single "Gasolina" rockets into mainstream popularity in the US, marking the rise of reggaeton in the US.

1990 In Puerto Rico, DJs inspired by Panamanian reggae begin to produce their own music.

1996 Tupac Shakur is killed in Las Vegas.

2003 For the first time, the top ten artists on the *Billboard* charts are all African American. Notably, they are all part of the Dirty South.

1992 DJ Playero releases his mixtape *32*, which has some of the earliest examples of reggaeton recorded, including a track by Daddy Yankee.

2001 Russell Simmons founds the Hip-hop Action Network.

2007 Numerous hip-hop artists perform at the Live Earth concerts, which take place around the globe.

Over the years, the Black Eyed Peas' skills have brought them to many red-carpet events. Whether it's the Soul Train Music Awards or a charity event, the Peas are often asked to participate.

The Importance of Political Involvement

In November of 2004, the country was faced with a major presidential election, deciding whether to reelect George W. Bush as president of the United States, or to elect John Kerry, a senator from Massachusetts. In late October of 2004, a couple of weeks before the actual election, the Black Eyed Peas flew down to Florida, where they held a benefit concert to encourage young people in the area to vote. Interrupting a tour in Australia to come speak to these young voters, the group stressed the importance of voting and the fact that their votes could be a force for change in the country.

will.i.am, the lead singer of the group, told students, "We need a change, y'all. Remember, your choice not only affects you, it affects the whole world." His words, and the music the group played, inspired these young adults to go and vote in the hope that they might be able to make a difference in the world.

In the 2004 election, many musicians and entertainment artists, including numerous hip-hop stars, used their talents to convince people to vote, mostly in support of the Democratic Party. Many concerts were held, especially in swing states, not only to entertain listeners, but also to promote voting and to shine the light on some important issues. The Black Eyed Peas were among these groups. David Niven, a political scientist, told Tania Valdemoro of the *South Florida Sun-Sentinel*'s Miami Bureau his opinions as to why so many performers are supporting the Democratic Party; "The Republican's sales pitch is about toughness," he said, "while the Democrat's sales pitch is about compassion. There just aren't many entertainers that support that Republicans' ideas." He went on to say that he is doubtful that these musicians, including the Black Eyed Peas, will be successful in changing anyone's mind about who to vote for. Instead, where they do the most good is in gaining attention. For example, while the Black Eyed Peas may not be able to convince anyone to vote for the Democratic Party who wouldn't have already, they can get the news out about the importance of voting, a constitutional right many people don't take advantage of.

will.i.am, on the other hand, disagrees with Niven's analysis. He thinks that he and other musicians are able to make a difference by convincing people to look at the issues at stake. In the same *Sun-Sentinel* article, he said:

> *"If a person sees that he can relate to my lifestyle, music, and viewpoints, he will listen to me. From the war to gay rights to women's choice, young people know what's right from wrong. Convincing them is a step-by-step process."*

Where Is the Love?

American politics isn't the only issue that the band deals with, both in its music and through their actions; they address other large issues as well. One of their most famous songs, "Where Is the Love?" was written in response to the state of the world after the terrorist attacks on September 11, 2001. In the song, the band pleads for a spirit of greater understanding and love throughout the world. In an interview with *USA Today*, will.i.am talked about the motivation behind the song, saying, "We were all just asking questions: Why would somebody do that? What did we do? It felt like that's what all America was thinking." The Black Eyed Peas try to convey their personal beliefs through their music, not only about the country's politics, but also about the state of the world.

The band's most recent world issue has been the environment. On July 7, 2007, the Black Eyed Peas, along with dozens of other musicians, participated in a Live Earth, a worldwide benefit concert. Performances were held all over the world, on every continent, including Antarctica, and all the money that was raised went to environmental research. Live Earth also tried to raise awareness about how ordinary people can make a difference and help stop hurting the environment, offering tips on its Web site about how to lower energy consumption through such everyday measures as changing lightbulbs or recycling.

The Black Eyed Peas played at the Live Earth concert in London, performing hits like "Where Is the Love?" "Let's Get It Started," and "Don't Phunk with My Heart." They also played a new song, "Help Us Out," that will.i.am had written for the concert, and another, known as "apl.de.ap's theme," which apl.de.ap had written only a few days before, after meeting Al Gore (author of *An Inconvenient Truth*)

The Black Eyed Peas and many other artists participated in the Live Earth concert series on July 7, 2007. The concerts helped bring attention to global warming and other environmental issues facing the Earth.

in Brazil. When asked about his new *a cappella* song, he said:

> *"Two days ago I had the blessing of being in Brazil, it's a beautiful place. When I think of planet Earth I think of Brazil because 20 percent of the world's oxygen comes from that place."*

The Black Eyed Peas have come a long way since their humble beginnings. However, some things never change; the band has always stressed social consciousness in their songs and lyrics. Because of this, and because of their unusual image, they are different from many other hip-hop artists, who often rap about violence or other negative issues. This difference is not a new thing—the members of the Black Eyed Peas have always been unique.

O.W. HOLMES JR HIGH
1220 DREXEL DRIVE
DAVIS, CA 95616-2123

One of the original members of the Black Eyed Peas was William Adams, will.i.am. His success isn't limited to his involvement with the Peas, however. Many other artists have taken advantage of his talents as well.

Beginnings

The Black Eyed Peas are a **diverse** group of people, with each of its members having a different *ethnic* background. However, they do have one thing in common—a love for hip-hop. It was this passion that led William Adams and Allen Pineda to form a band in high school, a group that has grown throughout the years to become known as the Black Eyed Peas.

William and Allen

William James Adams Jr., born March 15, 1975, is better known today as will.i.am. He was an only child, raised in the projects of East Los Angeles by a single mother; he has no memory of his father. He remembers that his mom never let him play with the other children in the neighborhood. Perhaps because of this, William grew up different from everyone else, wearing clothes that were a little odd. He was also quieter and more artistic than his peers. He also had a more *multicultural* background than many of the other children probably did: he was black, but he lived in a neighborhood that consisted mainly of Mexican immigrants; he attended an all-black church, but he rode the bus to a school attended by mostly white students. In an interview with *Blender* magazine, he talked about the diversity in his school and the influence it had on his later life:

> *"The black people hung out by the lunch tables, the Mexicans hung out by the bathroom, the white people hung out in their cars, the Asian people stood next to the lockers. . . . I would always wander between the different sections. If I didn't go to that school, Black Eyed Peas wouldn't be what it is. I don't think we would be able to relate to every country on the planet."*

Because of the variety of people William had the chance to interact with growing up, he was later able to relate to many different kinds of people. This skill helped him become best friends with Allen Pineda, a boy from the Philippines who didn't yet speak a word of English.

Allen Pineda, who later became known as apl.de.ap, was born on November 28, 1974, in the Philippines. His father was a U.S. serviceman who had left the country around the time Allen was born, so, like William, his mother raised him and his brothers and sisters alone. When he was young, he developed a condition known as nystagmus, which causes involuntary eye movements, and Joe Ben Hudgens, an American lawyer who had been sponsoring him, offered to adopt him and take him to the United States to live so he could get medical treatment. His mother agreed, and when he was fourteen years old, Allen moved to Los Angeles. It turned out that Hudgens' roommate was also William's uncle, and the two boys met and became good friends, even before Allen knew English.

In high school, William and Allen became part of a break dancing group known as Tribal Nation, which allowed them to take part in the hip-hop *culture* and to learn more about the music—lessons that were important in their later life.

Break Dancing

Break dancing has always been an important part of hip-hop culture. However, the earliest form of break dancing was not styled to hip-hop music, but instead developed in the late

will.i.am and apl.de.ap first got attention as members of Tribal Nation, busting moves like those of the break dancers in this photo. Break dancing began in New York City clubs, but the walls couldn't contain the b-boys' moves. Eventually, b-boys took their moves to the streets of New York City.

1960s and early 1970s in response to the disco music that was popular at that time. Break dancing would occur during the breaks in the music, when there were no lyrics, just rhythm.

The dance form quickly moved from the clubs to the streets. Rival gangs in the Bronx started holding break dancing competitions instead of fighting to resolve disputes over territories. But it wasn't until 1969 that break dancing became popular beyond the Bronx, when singer James Brown became popular and people started copying his energetic style of dancing during concerts. This was the "old style" of break dancing. Unlike the modern version of the dance, this break dancing did not involve any intricate gymnastics. Instead, it was only the feet that moved. While this might seem easier, it was actually more difficult because of the complex footwork and the complicated, extremely fast dance moves that were required.

Modern break dancing developed almost ten years later, in 1977. One break dancing group, the Rock-Steady Crew, combined gymnastics and martial arts with the traditional steps; this is similar to what break dancing is today. The modern form is a mostly unstructured form of dance, with much of the choreography *improvised* by the performer. It is incredibly disciplined, requiring tremendous strength and agility to follow the various steps.

Today, break dancing consists of five main kinds of moves. The first, toprock, is similar to the old style and involves only footwork. The dancer is in an upright position throughout these moves, and today it is used to work up agility before going into the more strenuous positions. The next type of move is downrock. This is similar to toprock, except it takes place while the dancer's hands and feet are both on the floor. Third are power moves, which are mostly borrowed from gymnastics, and require both speed and physical strength to carry out. Then there are freezes, which, as the name implies, involve the performer freezing while carrying out a power move. For example, a dancer could hold a handstand. The fifth type of break dancing move is called a suicide, where the performer makes it appear as if he has lost control of himself and falls on the floor. The more complicated and painful this looks, the more impressive the dancer's skills are seen to be, since he is actually doing this without hurting himself at all.

Break dancing has always been an important part of hip-hop, but some people are arguing that it is becoming less popular in recent days because of the rise in popularity of West Coast hip-hop. Some say that the more positive aspects of hip-hop culture, like break dancing, are being overpowered by the more negative aspects, like violence and sexism, which much of hip-hop encourages today. However, some artists like the Black Eyed Peas, still see break dancing as a means of enhancing their music and communicating what it means to them. In an interview with VH1, will.i.am talked about the importance of break dancing, as well as its decline:

> *"Break-dancing is like the sport of hip-hop. What we add to the dancing is the **spontaneity**, what the rhythm tells us to do. It's expression. But maybe a lot of cats don't want expression. In the public's eye, there's been a shift into what is marketable in hip-hop, and what's marketable isn't the dancers."*

While the importance of break dancing may be decreasing in much of the hip hop world, it is still an important part of the Black Eyed Peas, and has been ever since will.i.am and apl.de.ap were in Tribal Nation together as teenagers.

The Black Eyed Peas

When William and Allen got to their late teens, they decided to leave Tribal Nation to focus on the making of the music itself, forming a band called Atban Klann with some of their friends. William had started going by will.1.x, and Allen had become apl.de.ap. Things looked good for the young band. They were

When apl.de.ap first came to the United States, he spoke no English. That didn't stop him from becoming friends with will.i.am, and
this friendship and shared love of music and performing sowed the
seeds for the Black Eyed Peas.

able to get a record deal with the producer Eazy-E and were getting ready to put out their first album. Then Eazy-E died from AIDS complications in 1995, and the production company shelved Atban Klann's album. Discouraged, the group disbanded. William and Allen remained friends, however, and soon they formed a new band, this one called the Black Eyed Peas. will.1.x became will.i.am, and a new member, Taboo, joined the group.

Taboo, like will.i.am and apl.de.ap, had lived a somewhat **unorthodox** childhood. While the other two had both been exposed to and lived in different cultures, Taboo had spent his whole life in a Latino neighborhood in East Los Angeles. Taboo was born Jaime Gomez on July 14, 1975, into a Mexican family, although his grandmother, his mother's mother, was Shoshone. He grew up speaking Spanish and didn't know much about his Native American heritage. He always loved music and dancing, though while he was growing up people sometimes made fun of him because he was a Mexican who wore gold chains and other hip-hop clothing.

Before Taboo joined the Black Eyed Peas, he was mostly a dancer. He met will.i.am and apl.de.ap at a club, and when he joined the new band, he finally had the chance to follow his passion and had somewhere to fit in. But the Black Eyed Peas would still have a few hard years before they hit it big.

Like many groups, the Black Eyed Peas had growing pains, which included a variety of lineups. In time, the Peas settled on the members that would bring the group fame—and mega sales.

Early Music

The Black Eyed Peas didn't become an international sensation until the release of their third album. In fact, many people don't realize that their first two albums even exist. However, these albums set the groundwork for what the band would later accomplish.

Behind the Front

In 1998, the band released its first album, *Behind the Front*. While the album enjoyed success with some fans of **underground** hip-hop, it didn't make it into the public eye. It was clear to those who heard the album, though, that this band was different from most other hip-hop groups of the time. Instead of singing about drugs or violence, the Black Eyed Peas instead wrote and performed songs about social issues while maintaining a spirit of fun throughout the album.

One song, "Fallin' Up," dealt with the difference between what the Black Eyed Peas were doing and how other hip-hop performers saw them. The band talked about their unwillingness to follow trends and how they dealt with the negative reviews and publicity they were receiving. The lyrics in this album, according to Taboo, were written so that everyone could identify with them—in an interview with UGO.com, he said, "We

From the beginning, the Black Eyed Peas were different from most of the other hip-hop artists. And it was a difference they were proud of. According to Taboo, they wanted the average listener—not just someone clued into the hip-hop scene—to be able to understand their lyrics.

made songs that could be understood by the normal listener, where you don't have to be a part of the [hip-hop] scene to understand what we're talking about."

Not only were the songs easy to understand, they were also easy for people of different backgrounds to identify with. Part of the Black Eyed Peas' appeal has always been the fact that the group consists of people from different cultures—will.i.am is African American, apl.de.ap is Filipino, and Taboo is Mexican and Native American. Perhaps because of this, their music has always embraced cultural differences and found the similarities between them. apl.de.ap talked about *Behind the Front* in the UGO.com interview, saying that he believed the album appealed to people "not only because of the live sound, but because our music crosses musical boundaries as well as cultural boundaries."

While few other hip-hop bands have focused on the same kind of issues as the Black Eyed Peas, there are a few who have stressed social awareness in their songs and lyrics. Among these bands is A Tribe Called Quest, to whom the Black Eyed Peas have often been compared.

A Tribe Called Quest

Three high school friends—Q-Tip, Phife Dawg, and DJ Ali Shaheed Muhammad—formed A Tribe Called Quest in 1988. In the early 1990s, when they were putting out albums, most other hip-hop groups were focusing on issues like drugs or violence. This made A Tribe Called Quest the exception. Instead of focusing on the negative issues in the hip-hop world, they tried to make a difference and expose some of the more social issues. Their songs dealt with such problems as date rape, the use of the "n word" in black culture, and the problems with dealing with the rap industry. Talking about the reasons they made their album, *The Love Movement*, which focused on all the different kinds of love in the world, Muhammad told *Interview*, "It was just something that was needed. People are getting too much of the vainglorious stuff, and everything is about materialism, not love. Like Stevie Wonder said, love's in need of love today because there's so much hatred goin' round."

While they were completely different from most other rappers, A Tribe Called Quest still managed to be extremely successful, putting out more than ten albums during their ten-year career. Perhaps Ali Shaheed Muhammad was right—people did feel the need to hear about the importance of love, rather than the sex and hate that many other hip-hop artists were preaching. Regardless of the reasons the group was so successful, they were able to pave the way for other alternative hip-hop bands, including the Black Eyed Peas.

Bridging the Gap

In 2000, the Black Eyed Peas released their second album, *Bridging the Gap*. Like *Behind the Front*, this album also displayed the mix of cultures represented by the band. will.i.am talked to Silja Talvi of *LiP* magazine about what they hoped to accomplish with this album:

> "We thought along the lines of music and what hip-hop music has done culturally. It's crossed cultures, boundaries, musical **genres**. . . . With the exception of rock and jazz, it's the most diverse music as far as what it accomplished and has achieved as far as exposure."

On the album, the Black Eyed Peas highlighted the connections between different peoples through the use of hip-hop, but also the connections between hip-hop and other sorts of music. The album stretched the traditional definition of hip-hop, blending it with rock. The final product was an album that appealed to fans of both rock and hip-hop.

The Black Eyed Peas have been compared to A Tribe Called Quest. This group and its members, including Q-Tip, didn't focus on the negative parts of hip-hop. Their songs dealt with social issues, subjects that didn't attract many hip-hop artists of the time.

Although *Bridging the Gap* did have fans, it sold even fewer copies than *Behind the Front*. Things didn't look good for the band. apl.de.ap and Taboo started having problems with drugs and alcohol, and their lives could very easily have fallen apart. In an interview with *Blender*, will.i.am, talking about this period in their lives, said,

"I'd be like, 'Look at that homeless person over there. I wonder what decisions he made to get to that point?' I think if we didn't get through that whole period then we would probably all be homeless, mentally [disturbed] alcoholics, with no way out."

The Problem with Drugs

After the release of their second album, the band took a break for a while, and apl.de.ap started going through a rough patch. He got a letter from the Philippines, telling him that his brother had committed suicide. Then he went through a tough break-up with his girlfriend. In his depression, he turned to drugs, specifically to crystal meth.

Worried about the turn apl.de.ap's life had taken, his manager tricked him into signing into rehab. He told apl.de.ap they were driving to a thrift store to go shopping, and then headed to a clinic. While apl.de.ap argued with his manager at first, in time he came to see that he had a problem, and he stayed in rehab for a few months. This didn't completely solve the problem, and shortly after he came out of the clinic, he started doing drugs again. He went back into rehab again, and the second time he came out, he stayed clean.

At the same time, Taboo, while not addicted to hard drugs, struggled with alcohol. The band needed something to shock them into cleaning up their act and getting back together. The shock came in the form of the death of the **R&B** singer Aaliyah, who died in a plane crash in August of 2001. This, followed only weeks later by the terrorist attacks of September 11, reminded the band that they would not live forever. Before this, will.i.am had been writing songs that involved little more than interesting wordplay, but he decided then that something else was needed. He told *Blender*, "Then 9/11 came, and who [cares] about my grills and skills? We got to strike people's emotions, we got to hit them [in the heart]."

After this realization, the Black Eyed Peas got serious about their music. They began working on what would become their first hit single, "Where Is the Love?" It was also at this point that they met Fergie, who would become an important force in the band.

Young Stacy Ferguson began her career as a cartoon vo-cal artist, moved on to become an actress, and eventually became part of an all-girl band. But she didn't find phenom-enal success until she became Fergie and joined the Black Eyed Peas—a decision that no one regrets.

4

Stacy Ferguson

Stacy Ferguson, better known as Fergie, was born in Whittier, California, to two Catholic teachers on March 27, 1975. Her father was a vice principal as well as a football coach and geography teacher, while her mother taught special education and was a speech therapist. Fergie grew up loving to perform. Her mom described her childhood in an interview with *Rolling Stone*, saying, "She was always dancing for everyone. We'd go to the county fair and she wasn't in the shows or anything, but she'd just hop up on a makeshift stage and sing and dance." From the age of seven, Fergie knew that she wanted to be a singer, and she made sure that this dream became a reality.

Fergie's Early Career

Fergie started working in television when she was only eight, performing on television commercials, and then for a time as the voice of Lucy in Charlie Brown. She also appeared occasionally on shows like *Married with Children*. The role that influenced her future the most, however, was on *Kids Incorporated*, a sitcom dealing with issues such as friendships and divorce and featuring pop performances by the child actors.

Though Wild Orchard cut a couple of albums, neither was particularly memorable. Fergie wanted to leave the group, but she didn't want to hurt the other members. So she stayed, a decision that played a role in Fergie's drug abuse.

In a 2006 interview with *Rolling Stone*, Fergie talked about how the *Kids Incorporated* job forced her to grow up:

"In Kids Incorporated, I'm in the studio at eight years old, behind a microphone, learning the techniques. I was a little adult. I had to be professional on the set—you can't break out into a tantrum, so I learned. I always wanted to appease and put on a strong face and not let anyone know if there was something bothering me."

It was through *Kids Incorporated* that she found a way to start her musical career. Though she left the show in 1989, when she was fourteen, in her early twenties she and two other girls from *Kids Incorporated* formed their own band, Wild Orchid.

Wild Orchid

While Wild Orchid released two albums, neither of them did very well. Fergie was ready to leave and jump-start her own solo career, but she was used to living to please others, and she didn't know how to leave without hurting the other band members. So, not knowing what else to do, she stayed. This took a toll on her, as she became more and more depressed. Finally, she turned to drugs for relief, especially ecstasy. In an interview with *Rolling Stone*, she talked about her road to addiction:

"It started on the weekends and graduated to all the time. Me and my girlfriends would get ready, go out to the club, come home, change into my faux-fur coats and my sunglasses and rent a limo—spending all my child-actor money—and go to the club Garage that would start at 6 a.m. and dance till 12. Then I graduated to crystal. . . . It became less of a fun thing and more of a habit."

She couldn't hide her addiction forever. Fergie's band-mates and family found out about her drug problem when she started losing huge amounts of weight. Her mother didn't think anything was wrong at first. "I noticed her losing a lot of weight," she told *Rolling Stone*. "I was like, 'Wow. Good for you. Wish I could do that.' And then it started to be more and more, and it was, 'Are you OK?'" Forced to give some explanation, Fergie told her friends and family that she had an eating disorder called bulimia, hoping to get them off her back.

Finally, Fergie realized that she needed help; she was losing her sense of who she was. To get back on track, she stayed at the house of an ex-boyfriend for a couple weeks. He helped her detox, and then she dropped out of Wild Orchid and moved in with her parents. She told everyone the truth—which they had already guessed in spite of her explanations about bulimia—and she has remained drug free ever since. Kicking the drug habit was a major turning point for Fergie, but she still had some hard times ahead before things started to get better.

Becoming a Black Eyed Pea

While Fergie was now off crystal meth, her life still wasn't easy. She had gone into tremendous debt because of the difficulties of financing a drug habit. All the money that she had saved up as a child actor and put into a trust fund for her future was now used to pay her credit-card debt of tens of thousands of dollars. For the first time, Fergie didn't have all the money she needed. "I started living off unemployment and hustling," she told *Rolling Stone*, "getting my grind on, seeing if there were any writers I could work with, any home studios I could get into." Luckily for her, it was just at this time that the Black Eyed Peas decided they needed a new sound.

will.i.am decided he needed a female voice to sing with the band for the song "Shut Up" that appeared on the album *El-*

ephunk. A friend suggested that he talk to Fergie—that she would have the sound he was looking for. will.i.am had met Fergie before, when Wild Orchid had opened for the Black Eyed Peas at a concert, and he remembered that she had told him she was planning to leave the band. When he called her into the studio to hear how she sounded, he was impressed by her voice and her knowledge of music. He immediately offered her a job.

As Fergie started spending time with the other members of the Black Eyed Peas, working together and hanging out, they became good friends, and eventually she became a fixture of the group. They're like a family now. They may tease each other mercilessly, but they will always be there for each other when things get tough. When Taboo was asked, in an interview with LiveDaily.com, what he felt Fergie had brought to the band, he said:

> *"A lot of bags. Man, she had like 50 bags on the tour bus. She brought a lot of bags and a lot of makeup and a lot of hair products. A lot of girlie things. More than we expected. Nah, actually, Fergie has brought a resurgence to the band. . . . We've always had women in our songs, but now there's a face behind it. She also brings a very exciting energy on the tour bus. She's kind of—she's like a little sister of us, but by the same token, she's also like the mother. She takes care of everybody. If you're hurt, she'll nurture you. But we look after her like a sister."*

The group's closeness has been obvious, both in their music and in their everyday life. The addition of Fergie to the band has made them more of a family, but it also wasn't until Fergie joined the Black Eyed Peas that the group became an international success.

When things are meant to be, they are meant to be. Once Fergie joined the Black Eyed Peas, the group's success skyrocketed. The Peas (right to left)—Fergie, apl.de.ap, will.i.am, and Taboo—are more than a group, though. They are family.

Becoming Internationally Famous

Once Fergie had become a part of the band, the Black Eyed Peas recorded the song that would catapult them from a little-known alternative hip-hop band to an international sensation. "Where Is the Love?" was their breakthrough single, becoming the group's first top-10 hit. The song talked about the state of the world after the terrorist attacks of September 11, 2001, the war following them, and the lack of understanding between people. The band pleads for help, saying, "Father, Father help us/Need some guidance from above/'Cause these people got me questioning/Where is the love?"

The recording of "Where Is the Love?" took a year to complete as the group worked with Ron Fair, an executive from A&M Records, to shape the song into a hit. Justin Timberlake also worked with the group, writing the chorus and singing on the recording. The process was begun before Fergie joined the Black Eyed Peas, but when she became a part of the group, she was included. The band also added a live orchestra, an unusual undertaking for a hip-hop band. While many hip-hop artists would have shied at working with such a different sound, the Black Eyed Peas took it in stride. In an interview with VH1, Taboo said, "We like to utilize different types of instruments, whether it's a 40-piece orchestra, a tuba, a Theremin, or a kazoo." In the same interview, will.i.am tells a story about how they met a street musician playing the bagpipes in Australia. The band ended up taking him along with them on tour, and he opened several shows for them with his bagpipe.

The Black Eyed Peas used the success of "Where Is the Love?" to fuel the publicity for their next album, *Elephunk*, which would feature the song. Unlike their first two albums, which many people didn't even know existed, the band's next two albums would be instant hits around the world.

Elephunk

Elephunk, the first full album with Fergie as a member of the band, was a tremendous success. It sold 7.5 million copies around the world, and was nominated for four 2004 Grammy Awards, winning one for the Best Rap Performance by a Duo or Group for their song "Let's Get It Started." All of a sudden, the Black Eyed Peas were everywhere, their songs appearing in video games, on movie soundtracks, and in commercials. Their single "Hey Mama," for example, was featured on ads for the Apple iPod.

As on the Black Eyed Peas' earlier albums, social awareness and cultural values played a big part in the lyrics of *Elephunk*. While the most obvious example was in the song "Where Is the Love?" the values of the band members were clear in other songs as well. apl.de.ap's Filipino heritage is obvious in "The Apl Song," which he wrote about his life and country. He sings the song's chorus in his native language of Tagalog: "Listen,

"The Apl Song," written by apl.de.ap, is influenced by his Filipino heritage. The chorus is in Tagalog, his native language. apl.de.ap is very proud of his heritage and homeland.

I got a story to tell of all the events that have been going on in the promised land I was born in." He says the song was influenced by the folk songs of his childhood and deals with the culture and way of life of his homeland the Philippines.

With any album, some songs take longer to write than others. Just as "Where Is the Love?" had taken over a year to write, "It Smells Like Funk" also had a fairly intensive writing process. will.i.am talked about how he writes his songs in an interview with remixmag.com:

One of the group's earliest hits was "Where Is the Love?" They wrote the song after the September 11, 2001, terrorist attacks on the United States. The song was their way of dealing with the aftermath of the horrific events of that day.

"[I'm] always adding to [the music], just getting inspired by other things. On 'It Smells Like Funk,' I was listening to some Disney thing, and I liked the baritone men in it, so I was like, 'Oh, trombones! I want to use trombones! Nobody uses trombones and tubas.' So we came in and put the trombones and tubas on 'Smells like Funk.' . . . So we would always add to it."

While some songs were being constantly revised and changed, others, such as "Hey Mama," were written and produced in a day. will.i.am shrugs off this accomplishment, saying "It was just one of those days."

The music on *Elephunk* was more personal then many of the Black Eyed Peas earlier songs had been. The band was still recovering from all the issues that they had been dealing with, including their reactions to 9/11, and their lyrics reflect this. In an interview with Christina Fuoco for LiveDaily.com, Taboo talked about the difficulty of sharing such personal emotions in an album:

"It was difficult because it's hard to talk about your life, especially when you're going through breakups. . . . When I listen to 'Shut Up,' that song is about my relationship, right? When I think about it, I think, 'Wow. I created a song which was my actual life, and every time I listen to that song it always takes me back to that era when I was in a relationship.' So, yeah it is kind of hard sometimes. When I hear 'Words of Love,' I always think of 9/11 and how I felt that day when that happened. It works for us [to] bring out that emotion at that moment, to be able to present such a great emotional performance so that it's not just a fake performance. It actually has some validity and some form of reality behind it."

This is part of the band's appeal. Listeners can tell that they mean what they say; they are talking about real issues and things that matter to them and it shows in their lyrics and performances.

The tremendous success of their third album surprised the members of the Black Eyed Peas; in the interview for Live-Daily.com, Taboo said:

> *"When we make these records, we don't expect them to be No. 1. We don't expect the success of it because we go in thinking, 'This could be our last record so let's go out with a bang. Let's show the world we went out and we went out great.' Luckily, it's not going to be our last record. That's a great thing. I'm very excited, very blessed to have the opportunity to have the third album and for it to be as successful as it is, and ["Where Is the Love?"] to reach as many people as it has all over the world."*

After *Elephunk* came out, the Black Eyed Peas set off on an eighteen-month tour around the world. They estimate that they played 480 shows between June of 2003 and December of 2004. It was during this extended tour that their next album, *Monkey Business*, was written.

Monkey Business

In 2005, the Black Eyed Peas released *Monkey Business*. will.i.am explained the reasons for the title in an interview with Kylee Swenson for remixmag.com:

> *"The idea with Monkey Business was like organ grinders. You're working out there, and you only get a peanut, and you give all the money made to the monkey owner. There is a good payoff, but you work hard. Last week, we flew from South Africa to L.A. It*

was a 20-some-hour flight. And before that, we flew from Pittsburgh to Rome to Johannesburg, like, in five days. . . . I sound like a [jerk] to say that it's hard, but it is hard on your body when you are on three hours of sleep."

Because the album was written on the road, the band was forced to be faster and more efficient when producing it. Despite this, *Monkey Business* still manages to be as diverse as the rest of the Black Eyed Peas' albums, combining multiple music genres, including hip-hop, pop, soul, R&B, **funk**, and reggae. There were also many guest singers who were as varied as Sting, Justin Timberlake, and James Brown, three singers with completely different styles.

The longer the Black Eyed Peas stay together, the more comfortable they get, both with each other and with the music they perform. This is evident on *Monkey Business*, in which the songs were all written to show the styles of music the band likes to perform; on the Black Eyed Peas' Web site, will.i.am wrote:

"In going on the road for so long, we got an idea of what kind of music we wanted to play and make. Monkey Business is very much about the types of songs we play live. It's about a party. It's layered differently and has energy to it that reflects how we tour—from the beats to the types of instruments we used to how we interact with the audience. It's very much about us and the crowd on this record."

Listeners must have identified with the Black Eyed Peas' goals through this album: *Monkey Business* was even more successful than *Elephunk*. It went triple **platinum** and sold more than 9 million copies around the world. The album was nominated for four Grammy Awards, winning one for

Among those who helped turn "Where Is the Love?" into the Peas' first top-10 hit was Justin Timberlake. He wrote the song's chorus and even lent his voice to the record.

"Don't Phunk With My Heart." "My Humps" also took home a Grammy during the 2007 award ceremony, for the Best Pop Performance by a Duo or Group with Vocals.

While the Black Eyed Peas have had a very successful career as a band, and have no plans of breaking up in the near future, they are also each working on projects of their own. They believe in supporting each other as they find their individual voices, as much as they support each other while they work as a group.

They might not record as a group quite as often as they have before, but that doesn't mean the end of the Black Eyed Peas. They all participate on each other's solo projects. And they also spend time with charity projects, such as the Black Eyed Peas' Peapod Foundation.

The Future of the Black Eyed Peas

None of the Black Eyed Peas are ready to quit the band and embark on solo careers, but all four of them have side projects they continue to work on. Even though they are not working together as the Black Eyed Peas in these endeavors, they continue to support each other, no matter what the others are doing. They produce each others' solo albums and appear as guest artists on solo songs. And they continue to spend time together and tour as a group, even while they work on these solo projects.

will.i.am

will.i.am has a busy life outside of the Black Eyed Peas. He has his own record label, has released several solo albums, and is working on developing his own clothing line. i.am clothing, which is designed and developed by will.i.am, caters to both men and women. The clothes are distinctive, mirroring will.i.am's sense of personal style. Only a certain number of each piece of clothing is produced, guaranteeing that the look remains unique. In an article in *Remix* magazine, will.i.am said that "i.am clothing aims to fill the gap created in an industry where mass production consumes each person's need for individuality."

Then there is will.i.am's record label, will.i.am music group. He produces songs not only for his fellow band member Fergie, but also for people like Snoop Dogg and Diddy. will.i.am

Away from the Black Eyed Peas, will.i.am is keeping very busy. He has a clothing line, a record label, produces work for other performers, and writes and performs his own work.

was nominated for six Grammy Awards last year, and while some of these were for his work with the Black Eyed Peas, some, like his nomination for Producer of the Year, Non-Classical, were for his solo work.

Not only does will.i.am produce other people's songs, but he writes and performs his own as well. His first solo album, *Lost Change,* was released in 2001, and his second, *Must B 21*, came out in 2003. Neither album took very long to produce; in an interview with Corey Moss for MTV News, will.i.am said:

> *"The whole mind-set was if it takes longer than a week, don't put it out. If it's not done that day, throw it away and that was just it. It's not for radio, it's not for video, it's just for us to go out and make music that says, 'Oh wow, rewind that part, you wanna hear that!' That kind of stuff."*

While neither of will.i.am's first two solo albums sold very well, he claims that this was not his intent. Instead, his goal was to get his music out to those who would appreciate it, not to show the world his talent. He talked about his goals in producing some of his earlier work to *RIME* magazine:

> *"That's not really a lotta people—it's just tastemakers, people that care about music integrity. That's pretty much all I cared about. I got the video played on MTV—shot the video, paid for it myself, and I took it to MTV's offices and they added it. That was kinda surprising cuz it wasn't like [the album] was [selling] mad units, and there were a whole bunch of other groups that they weren't playing."*

Even though none of will.i.am's earlier work was expected to sell all that well, his third solo album, *Songs About Girls*, released in the second half of 2007, was a much more intensive undertaking. Guest artists like Nas and Snoop Dogg performed on the album, and, unlike his first two albums, will.i.am worked hard on marketing it and advertising its release. The first single from the album, "I Got It From My Mama," was released on July 20, 2007, with the video premiering on July 31. will.i.am has said that the album, as a whole, tells the story of the relationship between a girl and a boy, as they meet, fall in love, break up, and get back together. *Songs About Girls* is also more than a simple album. will.i.am told *Rolling Stone* that *Songs About Girls* was the "whole multimedia enchilada," including Web sites with Easter eggs and a film that follows the story of the album.

Fergie

Fergie's first solo album, *The Dutchess*, released in September of 2006, was a huge hit. The first three singles, "London Bridge," "Fergalicious," and "Glamorous" came in at #1, #2, and #1, respectively on the *Billboard* Hot 100. The success of the album was beyond Fergie's wildest dreams. In an interview with *Rolling Stone*, she talked about how it felt to be at the top of the charts:

> *"I looked at my Sidekick and it says, 'You're #1 on the Billboard Hot 100.' Going Number One on Billboard has been a dream for so long. I started crying, bawling really. It was a happy cry but . . . I felt like I was seven again. I started going over my life, all the ups and downs, everything that I've worked for. And finally this. It's ridiculous."*

The Dutchess has sold more than 3 million copies worldwide, and was certified platinum in May of 2007, quite a feat for the girl who was once nothing more than the singer in a failed pop group.

While Fergie has been working on her solo singing career, she has also experimented with acting. She played the part of the lounge singer in the 2006 film *Poseidon*. In the movie, she sings the song "I Won't Let You Fall," which she wrote with the help of will.i.am and the other members of the Black Eyed Peas. In 2007, she also had a small part in the movie *Grindhouse*.

apl.de.ap and Taboo

apl.de.ap and Taboo are both working on solo albums as well, although, as of early 2007, no album titles or release dates had been announced. They both want to embrace their native cultures, Taboo by releasing an album in Spanish and apl.de.ap not only by singing in his native language of Tagalog, but also by using more traditional Filipino instruments and musicians. While he is working on his solo album, apl.de.ap, like all the members of the Black Eyed Peas, still finds the time to be supportive of the other band members and their individual musical projects. They all encourage each other, despite the fact that the band is taking a break from recording at the moment. apl.de.ap talked to Marilyn Beck and Stacy Jenel Smith of the "Hollywood Exclusive" column about Fergie's new album, as well as his upcoming project, saying:

> *"Fergie's album's incredible. I'm really happy for her. Will has an album. I'm working on my solo project as well. I incorporated a lot of original Filipino instruments and mixed it up with hip-hop. We always help each other out even in our side projects."*

apl.de.ap, like will.i.am, has also started his own record label. His, called Jeepney Music Inc., was started to help native Filipino musicians produce their own music and to discover Filipino talents and help them to succeed in the music industry. In April of 2007, he had two musicians under his label, Replay and Rocky Rock, and was looking for more to send him samples of their work through the Jeepney Music MySpace site.

Taboo has branched out into other fields as well. He has had small parts in several movies, such as *Dirty*, a movie about ex-gang member police officers. He has also worked to set up a nonprofit school of the arts for kids in his hometown of Rosemead, California. The school would teach kids martial arts, break dancing, and music production. He sees the school

Taboo has pursued a solo career as well, including an album in Spanish. He's also started an acting career and a nonprofit school of the arts. Taboo knows it's important to give back to the community.

as a way to offer hope and a way out to kids growing up in a tough neighborhood.

Even as he tours and records, Taboo also tries to spend time with his son, Joshua, who was born when Taboo was only eighteen. Providing for his son is a big part of Taboo's life, and he says it has made him a more responsible person. It has also made him think about the way he looks at the world and what he wants to teach his son. He told *LiP* magazine that he wanted his son to learn about and understand other cultures, a value that all the members of the Black Eyed Peas share. While apl.de.ap sings about the Philippines, Taboo has worked toward embracing his Mexican heritage and culture. He is also interested, however, in learning more about his Native American roots.

Future Directions

The Black Eyed Peas might have been too busy lately to record another album together, but we have certainly not heard the last from the group. According to will.i.am, the band has a mission to spread hope to people through their music. He told *Blender*:

> *"We give people the tools to feel better about their lives when [stuff's] all [messed] up and you don't know what you're going to do with your life. I want to continue to do that for people, but at the same time there's a bigger goal. I just don't know what it is yet."*

Although the Black Eyed Peas may not know for sure exactly what they want to do at the moment, one thing is certain, they will continue to spread their views on the importance of love and acceptance of other peoples and cultures—something that is much needed in today's world.

**late
1960s–1970s**   Break dancing develops.

**Nov. 28,
1974**   Allen Pineda, apl.de.ap, is born.

**July 14,
1975**   Jaime Gomez, Taboo, is born.

**Mar. 15,
1975**   William Adams, will.i.am, is born.

**Mar. 27,
1975**   Stacy Ferguson, Fergie, is born.

1977   Modern break dancing develops.

1998   The group's first album is released.

2000   *Bridging the Gap*, the group's second album, is released.

2001   will.i.am's first solo album is released.

2003   "Where Is the Love" becomes the group's first top-10 hit.

2003   *Elephunk* is released, the first album to feature Fergie.

2004   The Black Eyed Peas perform in a series of concerts to encourage young people to vote.

2004   The Black Eyed Peas win their first Grammy Award.

2005   *Monkey Business* is released.

2005   The group establishes the Black Eyed Peas' Peapod Foundation.

2005   The group performs at Live 8.

2006   Fergie's first solo album is released.

2006   Fergie performs in the film Poseidon.

2007   Fergie appears in the film Grindhouse.

July 7, 2007   Black Eyed Peas perform at the London venue of the Live Earth concert series.

Albums

1998	*Behind the Front*
2000	*Bridging the Gap*
2003	*Elephunk*
2005	*Monkey Business*
2006	*Renegotiations: The Remixes*

DVDs

2004	*Behind the Bridge to Elephunk*
2006	*Live from Sydney to Vegas*
2007	*Black Eyed Peas*

Awards/Recognition

2004   Grammy Awards: Best Rap Performance by a Duo or Group ("Let's Get It Started").

2005   Grammy Awards: Best Rap Performance by a Duo or Group with Vocal ("Don't Phunk with My Heart").

2006 American Music Awards: Favorite Rap/Hip-Hop Group, Favorite Soul/Rhythm and Blues Group, Favorite Rap/Hip-Hop Album (*Monkey Business*); Grammy Awards: Best Pop Performance by a Duo or Group with Vocal ("My Humps").

Books

Bogdanov, Vladimir, Chris Woodstra, Steven Thomas Erlewine, and John Bush (eds.). *All Music Guide to Hip-Hop: The Definitive Guide to Rap and Hip-Hop*. San Francisco, Calif.: Backbeat Books, 2003.

Chang, Jeff. *Can't Stop Won't Stop: A History of the Hip-Hop Generation*. New York: Picador, 2005.

George, Nelson. *Hip Hop America*. New York: Penguin, 2005.

Kusek, Dave, and Gerd Leonhard. *The Future of Music: Manifesto for the Digital Music Revolution*. Boston, Mass.: Berkley Press, 2005.

Light, Alan (ed.). *The Vibe History of Hip Hop*. New York: Three Rivers Press, 1999.

Waters, Rosa. *Hip-Hop: A Short History*. Broomall, Pa.: Mason Crest, 2007.

Wells, Peggy Sue. *Fergie: Stacy Ferguson*. Hockessin, Del.: Mitchell Lane, 2007.

Web Sites

apl.de.ap
www.apl.de.ap.com

apl.de.ap
apl-de-ap.blackeyedpeas.com

Black Eyed Peas
www.vh1.com/artists/az/black-eyed-peas.jhtml

Black Eyed Peas Official Web Site
www.blackeyedpeas.com

Black Eyed Peas' Peapod Foundation
www.peapodfoundation.org

Fergie
fergie.blackeyedpeas.com

will.i.am
will.i.am.blackeyedpeas.com

Glossary

a cappella—Performed by voices only, no musical instrument accompaniment.

culture—The beliefs, customs, practices, and social behavior of a particular nation or people.

diverse—Made up of many different elements or kinds of things.

ethnic—Relating to a group or groups that share distinctive cultural traits.

funk—A style of music that derives from jazz, blues, and soul, and is characterized by a heavy rhythmic bass and backbeat.

genres—Categories into which artworks can be placed based on their style, media, and subject.

improvised—Made something up on the spot, without any preparation.

multicultural—Consisting of more than one culture.

platinum—A designation that signifies a recording has sold one million units.

R&B—Rhythm and blues; a style of music that combines elements of blues and jazz, and that was originally developed by African American musicians.

spontaneity—Behavior that is based on impulse, not planning.

underground—Separate from the main social or artistic environment.

unorthodox—Unconventional; out of the ordinary.

Index

About the Author

E. J. Sanna lives in Ohio and is currently pursuing her education in both environmental studies and religion. This is her third series writing for Mason Crest, and she enjoys other aspects of the publishing process as well.

Picture Credits

istockphotos: p. 40
    Silva, Daniel: p. 17
PR Photos: p. 32
    Alan, Scott: p. 24
    Harris, Glenn: p. 20, 30
    Hatcher, Chris: front cover, pp. 8, 36, 39, 48, 52
    Jue, Christopher: p. 12
    Lau, Tina: p. 2
    Mayer, Janet: p. 14
    Moore, Anthony: p. 22, 27
    Thompson, Terry: p. 46
    Wild 1: p. 44

To the best knowledge of the publisher, all other images are in the public domain. If any image has been inadvertently uncredited, please notify Harding House Publishing Service, Vestal, New York 13850, so that rectification can be made for future printings.